Table Of Contents

Introduction

Hear, O Israel: The LORD our God, the LORD is one. Love the LORD your God with all your heart and with all your soul and with all your strength. These commandments that I give you today are to be upon your hearts. Impress them on your children. Talk about them when you sit at home and when you walk along the road, when you lie down and when you get up. Tie them as symbols on your hands and bind them on your foreheads. Write them on the doorframes of your houses and on your gates.

— Deuteronomy 6:4-9

Impress God's Words upon your children! Find ways to include God's Word in your family's daily activities. Talk about what God says. Read. Understand. Memorize. Obey. These are challenging tasks for most parents and caregivers. In our minds we quickly say, "Yes, I know I should." But our busy schedules and endless demands often take over. Or we doubt our abilities to discuss and understand God's Word. And, if we're not careful, soon God's Word is set aside.

Bible Stories – is a new tool to help busy families learn God's Word while playing and enjoying time together.

First, the music CD features contemporary arrangements of traditional Bible songs and choruses kids have loved to sing for years! Incorporate the music into your daily schedule. Have your child awaken to the praise music or play it softly during breakfast. During drive-time turn off the radio and, instead, listen to **Bible Stories.** Play the music softly during a family meal. Plan an evening to sing together using the music CD. Or, send your young one off to sleep with the **Bible Stories** songs. Over time you'll easily develop a habit of incorporating great faith-building music into your family routine.

The fourteen **"I Can Read My Bible"** mini–books encourage young children to "read" their Bible regularly. Introduce the Bible story. Help them to cut out, color, and assemble their very own Bible storybook. Encourage your child to "read" the Bible to you throughout the day. Listen carefully as your child shares his or her understanding of the Scripture. Be prepared to ask age appropriate questions that will reinforce the facts of the biblical account. Have your child read the Bible while you read aloud or silently from your own Bible.

Our prayer is that God will richly bless your efforts to share God's Word with your young children.

Blessings,

Kim Thompson

Kim Mitzo Thompson

Karen Hilderbrand

Karen Mitzo Hilderbrand

I Can Read My Bible — Mini-Books

Instructions

Use these questions to talk about each story:

- What do you think the main character was thinking and feeling?

- What do you think others in the story were thinking and feeling?

- Why do you think God put this story in the Bible?

Included are fourteen "I Can Read My Bible" mini–books for you and your child to create and read together. Choose one story at a time –perhaps only one story per week. The Bible stories, Scripture references, and suggestions for teaching the value of each story are listed on the next page.

First, read the Bible story from your own Bible.
Next, learn the song from the music CD.

Finally, work together to create each "I Can Read My Bible" mini–book. Carefully separate the page along the perforation. Help your child color the illustrations on each page. Read each page together, helping pre-readers to sound out each word. Use the questions above to discuss the story and its meaning with your child.

Cut apart the pages of the "I Can Read My Bible" mini–book along the solid line. Each book has 8 pages. Put the pages in order with the cover on top. Staple the pages on the left side to make the book. Read and discuss the storybook throughout the week. Encourage your child to think about the story throughout the day and to share his thoughts with you or to ask questions he might have.

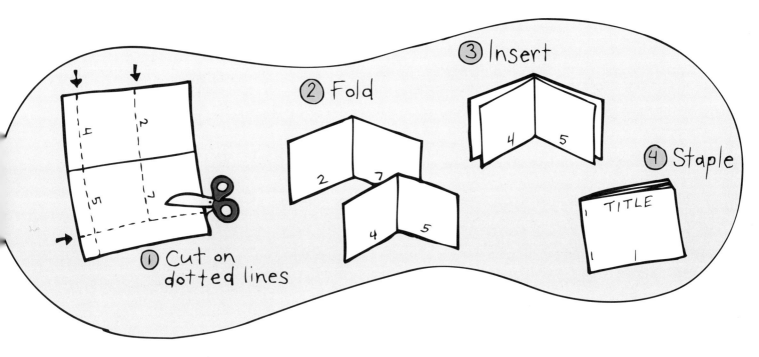

I Can Read My Bible — Mini-Books

SCRIPTURE	THEME	SONG	
In The Beginning **Genesis 1:1-31**	God wants us to thank Him for the wonderful world He made.	**Song: #4**	God Made Everything
Noah Obeys God **Genesis 6:9-22**	Noah obeyed God. God wants us to obey Him, too.	**Song: #5**	Who Built The Ark?
God Helps Joshua And The People **Joshua 6:1-21**	Joshua and the people obeyed God. God helped them win a battle.	**Song #6**	Joshua Fought The Battle Of Jericho.
The Lord Is My Shepherd **Psalm 23**	God is like a shepherd who cares for the sheep. God will take care of me.	**Song #7**	The Lord Is My Shepherd / Isn't He Wonderful?
God Helps Daniel **Daniel 6:6-28**	Daniel obeyed God. God protected Daniel.	**Song #8**	Who Did Swallow Jonah? (Verse 2)
Jonah Learns To Obey **Jonah 1:1-3:10**	Jonah did not want to obey God. He learns to obey God.	**Song #8**	Who Did Swallow Jonah?
God Sent Us A Savior **Luke 2:1-20**	God showed His love for us by sending Jesus.	**Song #9**	The Birthday Of A King
Jesus Loves The Little Children **Luke 18:15-17**	Jesus invited the children to come to Him. He loves all children.	**Song # 17**	Jesus Loves The Little Children / Jesus Loves Me
Jesus Visits A New Friend **Luke 19:1-10**	Jesus and Zacchaeus became friends. Jesus and I can become friends, too.	**Song # 11**	Zacchaeus
Jesus Wants Me To Obey **Matthew 7:24-27**	Jesus said a wise person will obey God and a foolish person will disobey God. I will be wise.	**Song # 10**	Wise Man, Foolish Man
Jesus Is The King **Luke 19:28-38**	Jesus enters Jerusalem and the people treat him as a king! I will treat Jesus as a king, too.	**Song: #12**	Blessed Be The Name / Ho, Ho, Ho, Hosanna
Jesus Died On A Cross **Mark 15:16-39**	Jesus died on a cross. Jesus is God's Son.	**Song: #13**	When I Survey The Wondrous Cross
Jesus Is Alive! **John 20:1-20**	God raised Jesus from the dead. Jesus is alive.	**Song: #14**	Alive, Alive
Peter And John Help A Stranger **Acts 3:1-10**	God made a man well. Many people worshipped God.	**Song #15**	Silver & Gold Have I None / My God Is So Big

In The Beginning
Genesis 1:1-31

1

God made the sky.
He made the sea.

3

FOLD

God made a man and a woman.

8

God made the sun.
He made the moon.

6

FOLD

5

"I will make the world," said God.
He made light and darkness.

2

God made the land.

4

God made the plants and trees.

5

God made big and small animals.

7

Noah Obeys God
Genesis 6:9-8:22

So God told Noah, "Make a boat."
Noah obeyed God.
3

Water went over the houses and trees.
6

Noah and his family were safe.
They said, "Thank you, God."
8

FOLD

FOLD

God was sad. Very few people loved Him.

2

Noah took his family and two of every animal on the boat.

4

Noah looked out of the boat. The water was gone.

7

God made it rain for many days.

5

God Helps Joshua And The People

Joshua 6:1-20

The walls of Jericho were very big. "God will help us," said Joshua.

3

God will help me, too.

8

Joshua and the people began to shout.

6

9

God led Joshua and the people to the city of Jericho.

2

Joshua and the people walked around the walls of Jericho. Then they went home.

4

The walls of Jericho fell down. "God helped us do this," Joshua said.

7

One day they walked around and around the walls seven times.

5

10

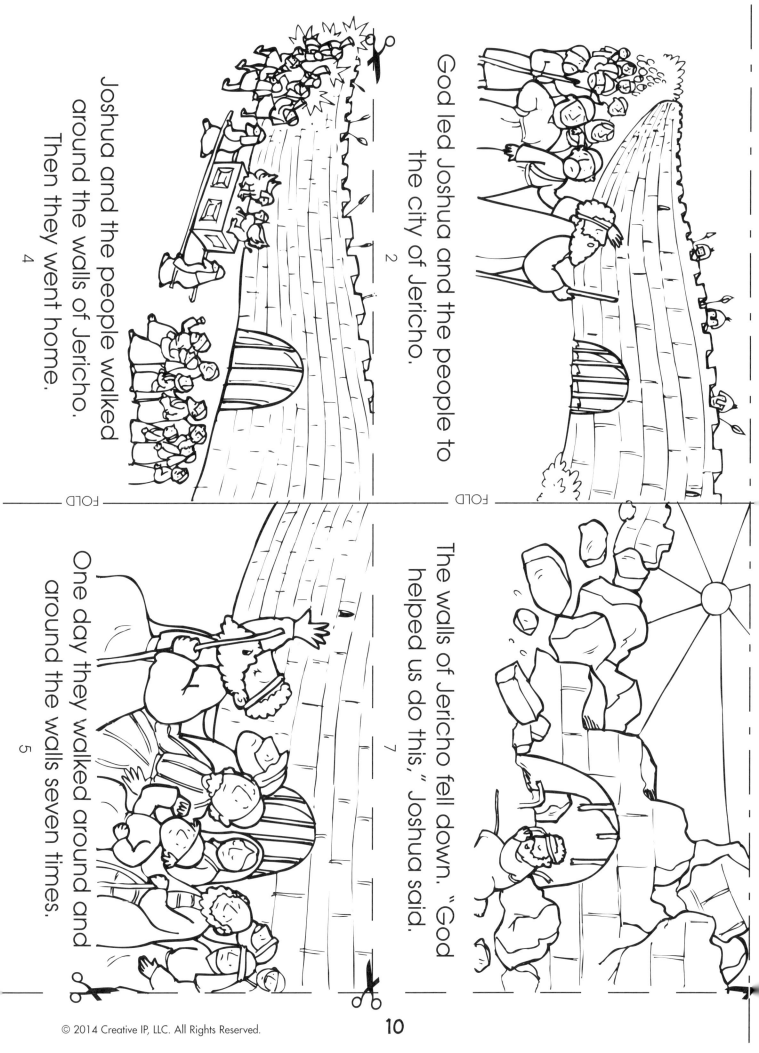

The Lord Is My Shepherd

Psalm 23

He lets me rest in the green meadows and by the peaceful streams.

3

FOLD

He will love me forever.

8

He gives me many good things.

6

11

The Lord is my shepherd. I have everything I need.

2

He guides me along the right paths.

4

He is close beside me. I will not be afraid.

5

He loves me every day.

7

God Helps Daniel
Daniel 6:6-28

Some men saw Daniel talking to God. They told the king.

"Bring Daniel out," said the king. "Everyone must love Daniel's God."

New Law
Everyone can love Daniel's God.
signed, King Darius

The next morning, the king went to the lions' den. "Are you alive, Daniel?" the king asked.

The king did not allow anyone to talk to God.

2

The king liked Daniel, but Daniel had disobeyed the rules.

4

The men put Daniel into the lions' den.

5

"Yes, my God closed each lion's mouth," said Daniel.

7

FOLD

FOLD

FOLD

I Law
No one can talk to God. Signed, King Darius

Jonah Learns To Obey

Jonah 1-3

Jonah said, "No," and sailed away on a big boat.

3

I will learn to obey God, too.

8

Jonah said to God, "I'm sorry." God told the fish, "Let Jonah out."

6

15

God told Jonah to go to Ninevah.

2

God sent a big storm. The men threw Jonah into the water.

4

Jonah woke up on dry land. Jonah obeyed God. He went to Ninevah.

7

God sent a big fish. The fish swallowed Jonah.

5

16

God Sent Us A Savior
Luke 2:1-20

FOLD

One day God sent an angel to Mary. "You will have a baby," said the angel. He will be the Son of God.

3

FOLD

The shepherds told everyone, "God sent us a Savior."

8

Mary and Joseph named the baby Jesus.

6

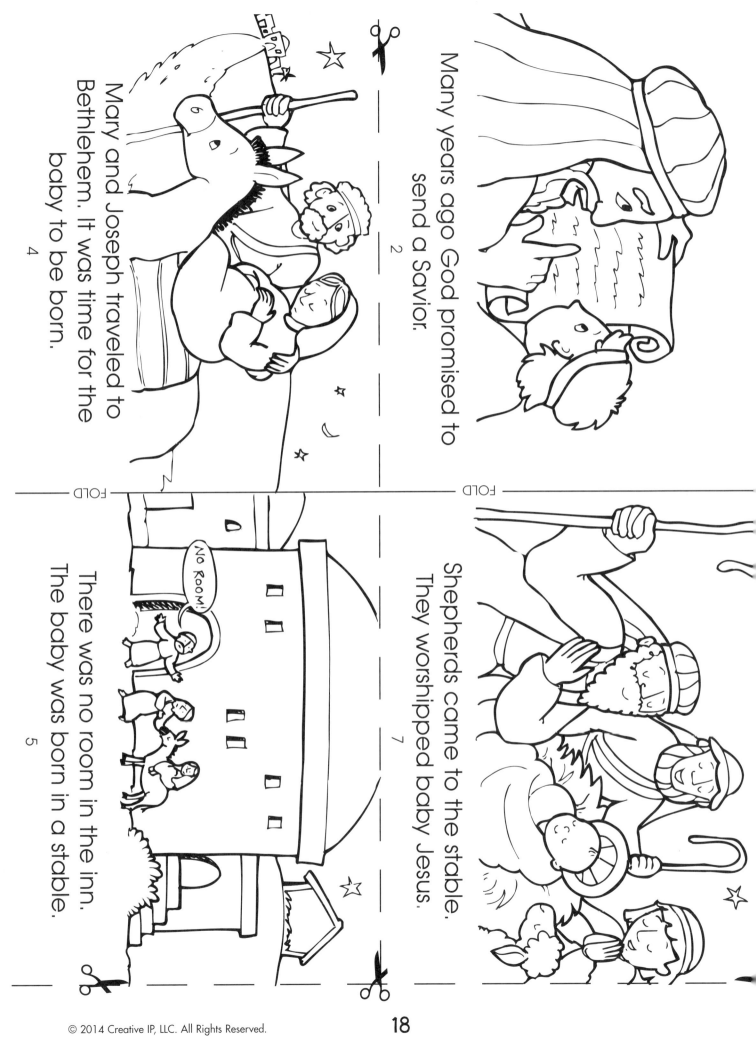

Many years ago God promised to send a Savior.

2

Mary and Joseph traveled to Bethlehem. It was time for the baby to be born.

4

Shepherds came to the stable. They worshipped baby Jesus.

7

No Room!

There was no room in the inn. The baby was born in a stable.

5

18

Jesus Loves The Little Children

Luke 18:15-17

Young children came to see Jesus, too.

3

Jesus talked to the children. Some sat on His lap.

6

"And I want you to love me, too," said Jesus.

8

FOLD

FOLD

19

One day Jesus was talking to many people. He was busy.

2

His friends tried to send the children away. Jesus stopped them.

4

"Let the children come to me," He said.

5

"I love each of you," He said to the children.

7

FOLD

FOLD

Jesus Visits A New Friend

Luke 19:1-10

Zacchaeus was a small man. He couldn't see Jesus.

3

Jesus is my friend, too.

8

"Come down, Zacchaeus," said Jesus. "I want to go to your house."

6

FOLD

1

Jesus was coming to town.
Many people wanted to see Jesus.

2

Zacchaeus climbed high into a tree.
Now he could see Jesus.

4

Zacchaeus climbed down from the tree.
Zacchaeus and Jesus became friends.

7

Jesus stopped at the tree.
He looked up at Zacchaeus.

5

Jesus Wants Me To Obey
Matthew 7:24-27

"A wise man built his house on the rock," Jesus said.

3

Jesus wants me to obey Him, too.

8

"Anyone who obeys me is just like the wise man," He said.

6

23

Jesus told a story to His friends.
"A foolish man built his house on sand," He said.

2

"Anyone who disobeys me is just like the foolish man," said Jesus.

7

"When the storm came, the house on the sand fell down."

4

"But the house on the rock did not fall," said Jesus.

5

FOLD

FOLD

Jesus Is The King

Luke 19:28-38

Jesus sent two friends into the city. They found a donkey and a colt.

3

FOLD

I will treat Jesus like a king, too.

8

Many people waved palm branches.

6

25

They took the animals to Jesus. He sat on the donkey and rode into town.

4

Jesus and His friends were traveling to Jerusalem.

2

The people shouted, "Hosanna!" The people treated Jesus like a king.

7

A large crowd of people came to see Jesus.

5

FOLD

FOLD

Jesus Died On A Cross
Mark 15:16-39

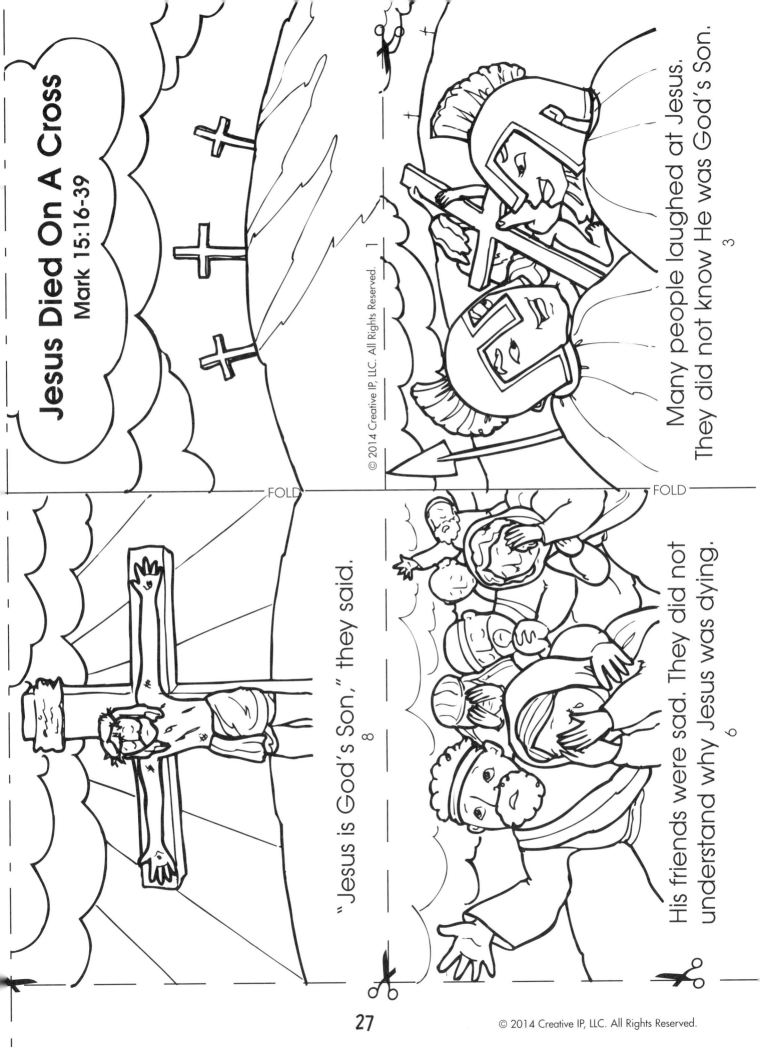

1

Many people laughed at Jesus. They did not know He was God's Son.

3

FOLD

FOLD

"Jesus is God's Son," they said.

8

His friends were sad. They did not understand why Jesus was dying.

6

27

Men put Jesus on a cross to die.
Jesus had not done anything wrong.

2

Jesus talked to God. "Forgive these
people," He said.

4

They put His body in the ground.
They sealed the tomb.

7

Jesus still loved the people.

5

Jesus Is Alive!
John 20:1-20

1

Mary looked inside the tomb. Jesus was not inside. Mary cried.

3

Soon, Jesus spoke to His other friends. Jesus was alive!

8

"Mary!" the man said. "Jesus!" said Mary.

6

29

Early Sunday morning Mary came to Jesus' tomb. An angel had rolled away the stone.

2

Mary saw a man in the garden. "Why are you crying?" He asked.

4

FOLD

Jesus was alive again!

7

"Someone has taken Jesus' body away," said Mary.

5

Peter And John Help A Stranger

Acts 3:1-10

Everyday a man sat by the gate.
The man could not walk.

3

Everyone in the temple was surprised.
Some worshipped God.

8

The man stood up and walked.
God had made the man well.

6

FOLD

FOLD

Peter and John were going
to the temple.

2

He asked Peter and John for money.
"We don't have any money," they said.

4

The man went into the temple.
He was jumping and praising God.

7

"But our God can help you,"
they said. "Stand up and walk."

5

✂

FOLD

FOLD

FOLD

✂

✂

Extra Fun Together
BIBLE STORY FINGER PUPPETS

Children love to present puppet shows for family and friends. Work together with your child to present your own Bible Story Puppet Theater with the simple finger puppets on pages 39 – 45. Cut out the finger puppets. To make each puppet sturdier glue the cutout to construction paper or poster board. You may even choose to laminate the puppets. Store the puppets in envelopes or plastic storage bags.

Mix and match the finger puppets to act out the Bible stories on pages 33 – 37. You'll find suggestions for simply explaining the Biblical events and their meaning to young children. For even more fun, see what other Bible stories you can retell using the finger puppets.

Be certain to also read the stories from your own Bible. Because parents or teachers often tell the Bible story from memory or from another book, children may not make the connection that the story is really from the Bible—not just another fairy tale or a good book from the library.

Bible Story Starters

Adam & Eve's Temptation – Genesis 3:1-13

Explain that Adam and Eve were permitted to eat from any tree in the garden except for one! Talk about why we might sometimes want to do what we've been told not to do.

Talk about the consequences of disobeying God, parents, teachers, and other authorities.

Noah Obeys God – Genesis 6:9- 9:17

Explain that no one had ever seen rain before! God asked Noah to build a boat because soon water would fall from the sky and cover the earth.

Talk about what Noah and his family might have thought while building the ark: What did they think about God? About the coming rain? About the people who were making fun of them for building a boat?

Abraham's Journey & Promise –
Genesis 12:1-5; 15:1-6

Explain that God told Abraham to pack all of his belongings and move his family. But God didn't tell Abraham where he and his family would one day live. Later, when Abraham and Sarah were very, very old, God promised that they would have a baby.

Talk about Abraham and Sarah's obedience even when God's instructions were very hard and sounded impossible.

God Takes Care Of Joseph –
Genesis 37:1-4; 18-28;
39:1-5; and 46:1-7

Explain that his brothers mistreated Joseph. Read Genesis 39:2. Talk about how God blessed Joseph, and allowed him to become a great leader in the country of Egypt. Many years later Joseph was reunited with his brothers and father when they moved to Egypt because of a famine. Talk about how God helped Joseph to forgive his brothers rather than hate them forever. Read Genesis 46:3 and discover what God's plan was for Joseph.

God Speaks To Moses –
Exodus 3:1 – 4:17

Explain that God protected Moses as a child and when he was older Moses became a leader in Egypt. One day, God asked Moses to lead His people out of Egypt to the land He had promised to give them.

Talk about how God had protected Moses as a child. (Exodus 2:1-10) What did Moses first think when God asked him to lead God's people? How did God convince Moses to obey Him? (Exodus 4:1-17)

Moses Leads The People
Out Of Egypt –
Exodus 12:31-39;
13:17- 14:31

Explain that Pharaoh—the king of Egypt—would not allow God's people to leave Egypt. Eventually, Pharaoh agreed to let the people leave, but he sent his armies after them. God protected Moses and the people as they crossed the Red Sea.

Talk about what it must have been like to walk through the Red Sea on dry ground with a wall of water on their right and their left. (Exodus 14:21-22) What did the Israelites think about God after seeing this miracle? (Exodus 14:31)

The Fall Of Jericho –
Joshua 5:13 – 6:21

Explain that God had led His people from Egypt, through the desert, and across the Jordan River into the land God had promised. Now God was going to help His people conquer the large, walled city that stood in their way. Talk about what the people of Jericho might have been thinking as they watched God's people march around the city every day for six days. What must it have been like for God's people to see the walls completely crumble? What about for the people of Jericho?

God Protects Daniel –
Daniel 6

Explain that as a young man, Daniel and his friends loved God. They were careful to do what God instructed. Soon the king of Babylon made Daniel a leader. But there were other men who wanted to get Daniel into trouble. (Daniel 6:3-5)

Talk about why these men tricked the king into passing a law against praying to anyone but the king. Why did Daniel disobey the king's law? What do you think the king thought when he learned Daniel had broken the law? What happened while Daniel was in the den of lions?

David Defeats Goliath –
1 Samuel 17:1-51

The Israelite soldiers and even the king were afraid of the giant Goliath. But David trusted God to help him defeat the giant who was mocking God.

Talk about why David's brothers and other soldiers thought David should not fight Goliath. Talk about what it must have been like for the army and the king to watch David walk onto the battlefield. What did Goliath think of David? Most importantly, what did David think about God?

Jesus Is Born –
Luke 2:1-20

Explain that God had planned to send His Son, Jesus, into the world. Talk about what it must have been like for Mary, Joseph, the innkeeper, the angels announcing Jesus' birth, the shepherds, and even Jesus himself leaving heaven to be born in Bethlehem. Why do you think God chose to send Jesus as a baby rather than as an adult king or soldier?

35

Jesus Chooses His Disciples – Mark 3:13-19

Explain that Jesus chose twelve men to be with Him as He traveled. Jesus taught them what God wanted them and us to know about Himself. They became Jesus' closest friends. The disciples were ordinary men—not necessarily rich or famous. Some were fishermen and one was a tax collector. Some had tempers. One even turned against Jesus. Talk about the type of people God might want to use to help Him today.

Jesus Walks On The Water – Matthew 14:22-33

Explain that Jesus told His disciples to go to the other side of the lake. He remained behind to pray. Later, He joined His disciples by walking on the water across the lake.

Talk about what the disciples thought when they saw someone walking on the water? (Matthew 14:26) How did Jesus respond? Out of the group of twelve men how many had faith enough to walk out to Jesus? The key point is found in verse 33.

The Parable Of The Lost Sheep – Luke 15:1-7

Explain that Jesus taught the people using simple stories. This story is one of three in this chapter about someone searching for a valuable item that was lost. Talk about what it must have been like to be a real shepherd searching for and finding one little sheep that wandered away. Jesus explains the story by saying that God is so happy when someone finally understands and asks God to forgive his or her sin.

Jesus Welcomes The Children – Mark 10:13-16

Explain that Jesus hugged the children and invited them to sit on His lap. Jesus explained to the adults that everyone must have the same kind of faith that a child has. Let your child talk to you openly about what he or she knows and believes about Jesus. Listen. You might discover exactly what Jesus was speaking of as He blessed the children in His arms.

Jesus Enters Jerusalem – Mark 11:1-11

Explain that Jesus understood He was entering Jerusalem for the last time before He would die on a cross. Jesus rode on the back of a donkey and crowds of people welcomed Him. The crowds were treating Jesus like they would treat a king. Talk about what Jesus might have been thinking as He heard the shouts and saw the waving palm branches. Jesus is a king, but is He the type of king the people really wanted? Why or why not?

Jesus Has Supper With His Friends – Matthew 26:26-29

Explain that it was almost time for Jesus to die on the cross. He had one last meal with His closest friends, the disciples. During that meal, Jesus used the bread and the drink to teach His friends about His death. What did Jesus say the bread would remind them of someday? What did Jesus say the drink would remind them of someday? Consider beginning to explain about the sacrament of communion as it is understood and practiced in your church.

Jesus Is Alive Again – John 20:1-9

Explain that Jesus' friends were sad after Jesus died. On Sunday morning His friends came to the place where Jesus was buried. But Jesus' body was not there! An angel appeared to some of the women and said, "Don't be afraid! He is risen just like He said!" Later, the friends saw Jesus alive.

Talk about how Jesus' friends must have felt before and after learning that Jesus was alive again. Explain that God raised Jesus from the dead.

Telling Others About Jesus – Acts 2:42-47

After Jesus died and was made alive again, Jesus' friends began to tell everyone in Jerusalem about Him. Jesus' friends spent a lot of time with each other. Peter and John spoke to large crowds of people about Jesus. Read Acts 2:47 and see what God was doing as Jesus' friends talked with others about Him.

Saul Decides To Follow Jesus – Acts 9:1-17

Saul did not like the people who believed Jesus was the Son of God. But one day, a bright light blinded Saul. He heard Jesus speaking from heaven. Saul got up and followed Jesus' instructions. Later, his name was changed from Saul to Paul. Paul became a great leader and traveled very far telling others all about Jesus. God used Paul to write many of the books in the New Testament. Talk about how different Saul was after learning more about who Jesus really is.

Paul And Silas In Jail – Acts 16:22-35

Explain that Paul and Silas were in jail because they were telling other people about Jesus. Paul and Silas sang and prayed loudly while they were in jail. Soon God caused the earth to shake and the prison doors to come open. Paul and Silas told the person in charge of the jail about Jesus. Soon the other leaders let Paul and Silas go free. Talk about why Paul and Silas were singing and praying in the jail. What do you think they were asking God to do? Do you think God answered their prayer?

37

Scripture

Song

#20 Standin' In The Need Of Prayer / Whisper A Prayer

Talk It Over

Don't worry! Pray! Simply stated, that's what God says in Philippians 4:6. The next verse says that God will respond by giving us peace and guarding our hearts and minds. Prayer is simply talking and listening to God. Kids— and families—can talk to Him about everything in life: family, friends, church, schoolwork, fears, questions. You can also pray for the needs of others.

- Use the following questions to talk with your child about prayer.

- Prayer is talking to God. How is prayer like making a telephone call or sending a message?

- Is there anything that I cannot talk to God about? Why or why not?

- Does God ALWAYS do what we want Him to do? Read Romans 8:28

Fun Together

FAMILY PRAYER JOURNAL

Encourage family prayer time by making a Family Prayer Journal in which your child writes or draws the requests your family brings to God. Keep the prayer journal on your dining table or in another place where everyone will see it often. Consider dating your requests, and then writing when and how God responded to the requests. Create family keepsakes by simply making another Family Prayer Journal when this one is complete. Save them and once a year or so read through the journals. You'll remember what your family has experienced together and have reason to celebrate God's faithfulness.

To make a Family Prayer Journal, fold several pieces of copy paper in half, making a booklet. Next, fold one sheet of construction paper in half. Insert the copy paper between the construction paper, fold-to-fold. Help your child place one hand on the paper, little finger on the fold. Trace around his hand. Holding all the papers together, cut out the hand. Do not cut on the fold. Punch two holes along the fold, thread yarn through the holes and tie it. On the cover write Family Prayer Journal and the date.

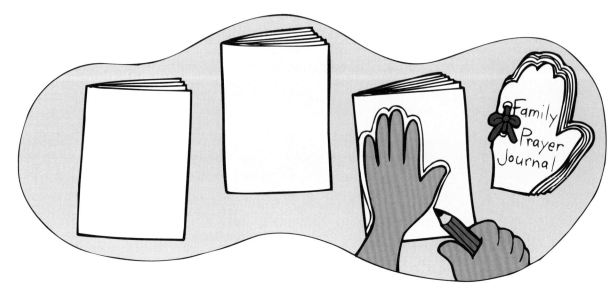

Mary

David

Joseph

Angel

Eve

Adam

Jesus

This page intentionally left blank for the "Finger Puppets" activity to be completed.

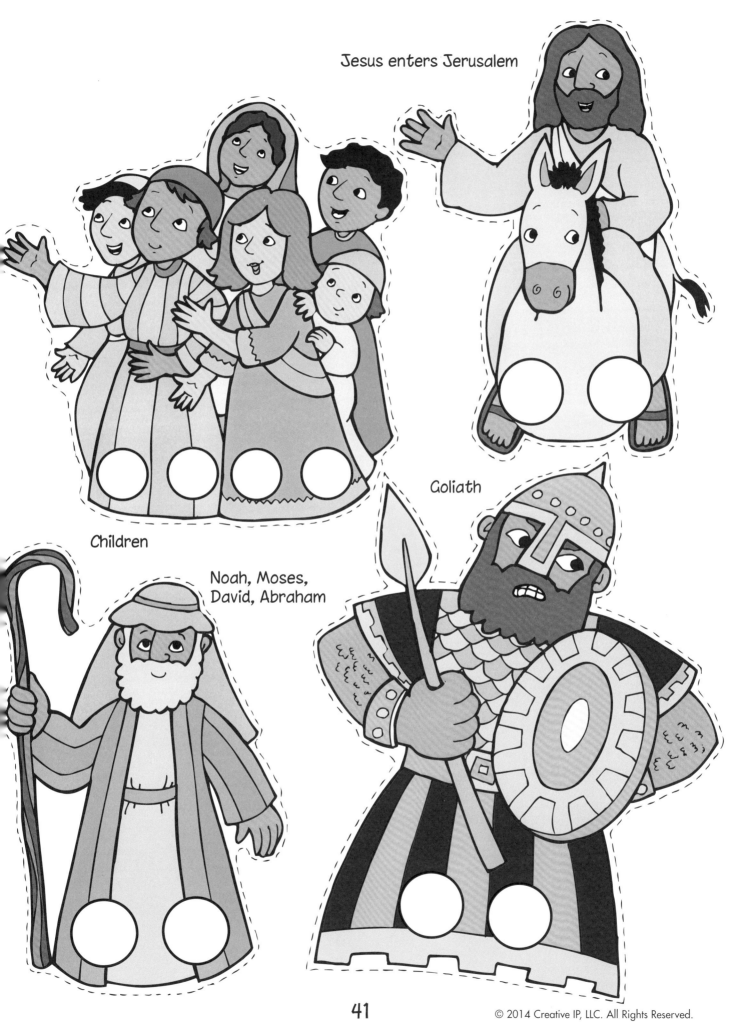

Jesus enters Jerusalem

Goliath

Children

Noah, Moses,
David, Abraham

41

This page intentionally left blank for the "Finger Puppets" activity to be completed.

Joseph

Crowd of People

Pharoah

Jesus

43

This page intentionally left blank for the "Finger Puppets" activity to be completed.

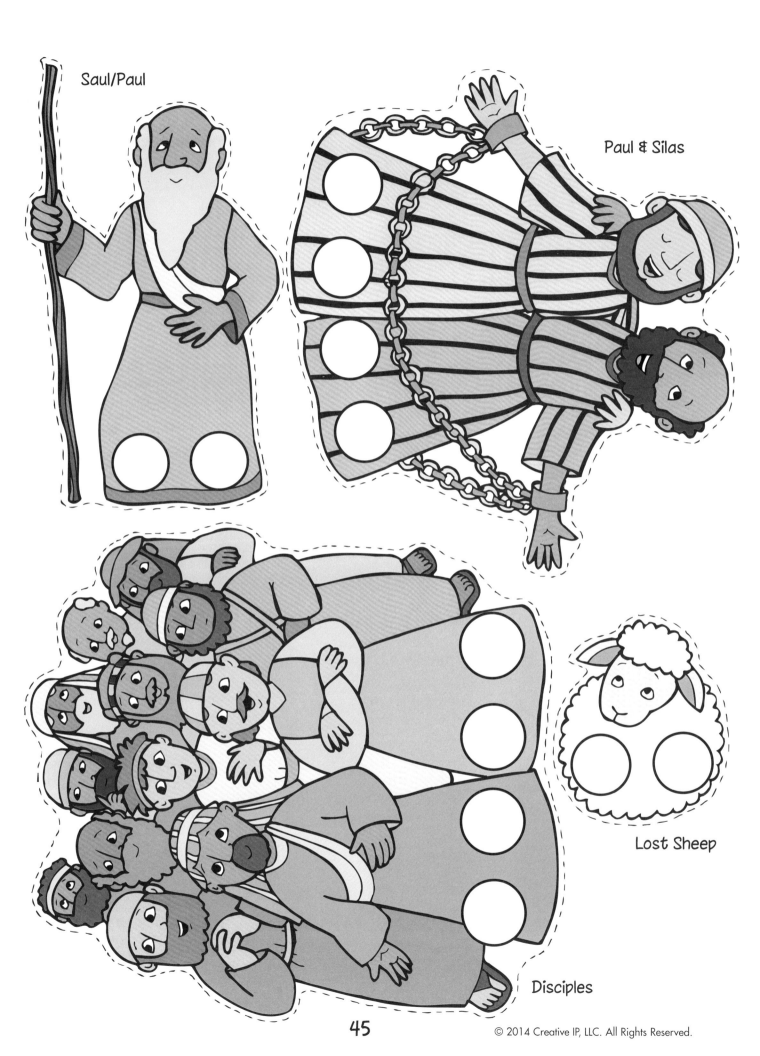

Saul/Paul

Paul & Silas

Lost Sheep

Disciples

45

This page intentionally left blank for the "Finger Puppets" activity to be completed.

Scripture

Philippians 4:7
And the peace of God, which transcends all understanding, will guard your hearts and your minds in Christ Jesus.

Song

#19 His Banner Over Me Is Love / I've Got Peace Like A River

Fun Together

HEAVENLY HUGS

Help your child trace each arm and hand on a large piece of construction paper. Cut each arm out. Tape, glue, or staple together the ends of each arm. Help your child write a favorite, comforting Bible promise on the outstretched arms. Here are suggestions:

- I will never leave you.
  –Joshua 1:5

- Peace I leave with you. Do not be afraid.
  –John 14:27

- Do not be worried about anything.
  –Philippians 4:6

Decorate the outstretched arms. When finished, roll the arms together. Then unroll the arms and wrap it around your child's waist—pretending it's a heavenly hug and promise from God.

For more fun, have each family member make a set of Heavenly Hugs. Place your child in charge of giving God's hugs to the other family members.

Talk It Over

Many parents will agree that simply giving a hurting child a hug goes a very long way toward making that child feel secure and loved. Imagine receiving a hug from God! Many Scriptures speak of God's unfailing love, His watchfulness and protection, His concern and compassion, and His willingness to comfort in hard times. Use these questions to talk with your child:

- When do you think a hug from me helps most?

- What do you think a hug from God might feel like?

- God doesn't come down and give us a real bear hug. How can God make us feel better?

I will never leave you. Joshua 1:5

47

Suggested Scripture Memory Verses

1. Proverbs 15:1 — A gentle answer turns away wrath, but a harsh word stirs up anger.

2. Philippians 2:5 — Your attitude should be the same as that of Christ Jesus.

3. Psalm 139:14 — I praise you because I am fearfully and wonderfully made.

4. Proverbs 3:5 — Trust in the LORD with all your heart and lean not on your own understanding.

5. Ephesians 4:32 — Be kind and compassionate to one another.

6. Philippians 2:14 — Do everything without complaining or arguing.

7. Philippians 4:13 — I can do everything through him who gives me strength.

8. Psalm 27:1 — The Lord is my light and my salvation—whom shall I fear?
The Lord is the stronghold of my life—of whom shall I be afraid?

9. Genesis 1:1 — In the beginning God created the heavens and the earth.

10. Psalm 24:1 — The earth is the LORD'S, and everything in it, the world, and all who live in it.

11. Luke 6:31 — Do to others as you would have them do to you.

12. Hebrews 11:1 — Now faith is being sure of what we hope for and certain of what we do not see.

13. Hebrews 13:8 — Jesus Christ is the same yesterday and today and forever.

14. John 11:25 — Jesus said to her, "I am the resurrection and the life.
He who believes in me will live, even though he dies.

15. Romans 12:9 — Love must be sincere. Hate what is evil; cling to what is good.

16. 2 Timothy 3:16 — All Scripture is God-breathed and is useful for teaching,
rebuking, correcting and training in righteousness.

17. Galatians 5:14 — The entire law is summed up in a single command: "Love your neighbor as yourself."

18. 1 Corinthians 13:4 — Love is patient, love is kind. It does not envy, it does not boast, it is not proud.

19. Luke 6:36 — Be merciful, just as your Father is merciful.

20. Luke 11:28 — He replied, "Blessed rather are those who hear the word of God and obey it."

21. Psalm 107:1 — Give thanks to the LORD, for he is good; his love endures forever.

22. Philippians 4:6 — Do not be anxious about anything, but in everything, by prayer and petition,
with thanksgiving, present your requests to God.

23. Romans 12:21 — Do not be overcome by evil, but overcome evil with good.

24. Psalm 119:11 — I have hidden your word in my heart that I might not sin against you.

25. Colossians 3:2 — Set your minds on things above, not on earthly things.